THE OFFICIAL
WEST BROMWICH ALBION
ANNUAL 2015

Written by Dave Bowler
Designed by Brian Thomson

A Grange Publication

© 2014 Published by Grange Communications Ltd., Edinburgh, under licence from West Bromwich Albion Football Club. Printed in the EU.

Photography © West Bromwich Albion Football Club and Action Images.

ISBN: 978-1-908925-74-9

£7.99

CONTENTS

ALAN IRVINE

Albion appointed Alan Irvine as our new Head Coach in June this year, the 55 year old Scot coming in to replace Pepe Mel.

"I'm absolutely delighted to get this job," said Irvine. "I've got a great deal of respect for the club, right the way from the first team through to the Academy.

"The situation at this club is similar to what I went through at Everton when I went there with David Moyes as his assistant.

"It is run very sensibly and, as a result of that, any head coach coming in has got a great

"My passion is for coaching and I believe my strength is on the training ground, which is where we need to get the work done."

Irvine will work closely with Albion's Technical Director Terry Burton and is determined to have a successful time at The Hawthorns.

"Terry is someone I've respected as a coach from a distance for many years and I'm looking forward to working closely with him," he added.

"The Hawthorns is a place I have visited many times as manager and assistant manager, and it is always difficult to get a result.

"The fans are extremely passionate, terrific in getting behind the team, and I'm sure it is a great place to work as a player or a coach.

"I'm extremely excited about the challenge and I'll certainly give it everything I possibly can.

"I'll work however many hours it takes to make

GOAL OF THE SEASON

Albion's goal of the season came almost from the kick-off in our big six-pointer against Cardiff City.

Morgan Amalfitano was running away to fetch a pass down the right. Without stopping to control it, without looking up, without even looking at goal, he put his right foot through the ball, and watched it loop up through the air, over the head of the Cardiff goalkeeper and into the far corner of the net.

Très bien Morgan, très bien.

SEASON REVIEW

2013-14

WEST BROMWICH ALBION

AUGUST:

There's nothing quite like the start of a new season to get everyone excited, especially after Albion finished the previous term in eighth place after drawing 5-5 with Manchester United on the last day. But the opening game against Southampton didn't have anything like as many goals in it, just one in the end – and it came at the wrong end of the pitch, a Lambert penalty.

After that we went to Goodison Park to take on Everton. Everything was going well until the last 15 minutes when Ben Foster suddenly had to limp off. After 10 years at the club, Luke Daniels finally made his debut – if at first you don't succeed, try, try again! – and kept Everton out so that we get a 0-0 draw.

Luke was in goal again when Newport County arrived at The Hawthorns for the Capital One Cup, a night when Saido Berahino made his first appearance for the Baggies and bagged himself a hat-trick to boot as we won 3-0.

SEPTEMBER:

Back to The Hawthorns for a less than super Sunday when Swansea ushered in September by beating Albion 2-0 in a game that was less than exciting. The following 24 hours more than made up for that though because on transfer deadline day, Stephane Sessegnon, Morgan Amalfitano and Victor Anichebe all signed up for the Albion.

Morgan and big Vic featured for the Baggies the following Saturday in London when we took on Fulham, but it was Gareth McAuley who was the hero of the hour, rising above everyone to power in a header in the last minute to give us our first league goal of the season and a precious 1-1 draw.

Stephane made his debut the week after, against his old club Sunderland. He didn't take long to make an impact either, scoring in Albion's 3-0 win that ended with Sunderland boss Paolo di Canio walking across The Hawthorns to talk to the Sunderland fans. It was his last chance – the Albion sacking curse worked again the following week!

We played a great Capital One Cup tie against Arsenal that midweek, Saido scoring again in a 1-1 draw, but sadly, we went out of the competition on penalties. Not that it seemed to matter three days later when we went to Manchester United and won 2-1 – our first victory at Old Trafford since Christmas 1978 when we won 5-3. It was a well deserved win too, Albion controlling the game, Saido Berahino putting us in front before Morgan Amalfitano won the game with a solo run from his own half. No wonder they call it the Theatre of Dreams!

OCTOBER:

Arsenal were at The Hawthorns for the second game in a row as we started October and an exciting game ended up 1-1 again after Claudio Yacob scored his first ever Albion goal – and didn't he celebrate it!

We travelled to Stoke next and came home with yet another draw, 0-0 this time, though it should have been much more. Youssouf Mulumbu was so badly fouled in the box that the Stoke man even dragged his boot off him, and still there was no penalty! A week later, it was the Luis Suarez show at Anfield as the striker grabbed a hat-trick for Liverpool as they beat us all too easily, 4-1.

NOVEMBER:

It was a big start to the month when struggling Crystal Palace arrived at The Hawthorns in what looked like a must win game for the Albion. So we did! Berahino and McAuley were on target for the Baggies and managerless Palace left the ground looking very relegated indeed...

Spirits were high as we headed off to Stamford Bridge and we put in a magnificent display that should have taken Jose Mourinho's unbeaten home record off him. Goals from Sessegnon and Shane Long gave us a 2-1 lead that extended deep into injury time before Ramires had a little lie down in the penalty area and the referee gave Chelsea a penalty. A 2-2 draw felt like we had lost the game and that one decision had a big impact on Albion's season.

Not that it looked that way when we tore into the Villa under the lights on a Monday night, chasing into a two goal lead in no time thanks to two goals from Long. Sessegnon could have made it 3-0 but in the second half, Villa came more and more into the game and scored two goals to force another 2-2 draw.

We were on the television again on the Saturday night, up at Newcastle United, a game we lost 2-1, Chris Brunt getting our goal.

DECEMBER:

It was lucky we had the coming of Christmas to take our minds off things because the start of December was pretty miserable. Manchester City came to The Hawthorns and played like champions to take a 3-0 lead, though we got a couple of late goals to make the scoreline look a bit better.

Fellow strugglers Norwich were up next in another really important home game but everything went wrong for the Baggies and we ended up beaten 2-0 and looking in big trouble. When we lost 1-0 at Cardiff a week later, it meant the end of Steve Clarke's time as the Albion's Head Coach.

Keith Downing took charge for the busy and important Christmas period but it didn't look as though it was going to start very well at all with Albion 1-0 down at home to Hull with only a few minutes to go. But Zoltan Gera found a perfect pass for Matej Vydra who smashed the ball in to get us a draw.

Then it was down to London for Christmas with a game against Spurs on Boxing Day and West Ham two days later. With Spurs under new management too in Tim Sherwood, it was a game that was hard to predict, but when in doubt with the Albion during this season, go for a draw. So we did, 1-1 thanks to a Jonas Olsson goal.

West Ham next and Nicolas Anelka finally scored for the club; Saido Berahino also getting a goal in a game that went from end to end before it finished up as a – you guessed it – draw, 3-3. What a way to finish the year.

JANUARY

New Year's Day brought a visit from Newcastle United and we were into another one of those must win games after all those draws. And win it we did, although it took a long time to get there. After pounding away at the Magpies without success, we got a late, late penalty and with nerves of steel, Saido stepped up to score with three minutes left.

We won't say much about the FA Cup tie against Crystal Palace, we lost a rotten game! Then it was on to Southampton where we were watched for the first time by incoming Head Coach - Pepe Mel. He saw us lose 1-0, then he had just over a week to prepare the team for some Monday night football and a fixture at home to the impressive Everton. Led by fellow Spaniard Roberto Martinez, Albion fans welcomed Romelu Lukaku back to The Hawthorns. In a high energy game, Albion recovered from being a goal down to win a point thanks to Diego Lugano's second half header.

Then we went to Villa Park… We were 2-0 up in nine minutes – sound familiar? – then 3-2 down after 37, before going in at 3-3 at half-time. The game was decided by a Benteke penalty in a quieter second half, but it was a pretty bad night all round for the Baggies.

FEBRUARY

The tough run of home games continued with Liverpool coming to The Hawthorns. We fell behind but some high energy pressing play forced Kolo Toure into an error and Victor Anichebe levelled things up.

Next it was off to the Palace – no, not to see the Queen, to see Tony Pulis. We had a dreadful first half and were losing 2-0 before we introduced Thievy at half time for his debut and he was on target inside a minute! Unfortunately, another awful refereeing decision gave Palace a penalty and they sealed the game with it.

Chelsea were next up and although Albion gave as good as they took, when Mourinho's men stole a goal in first half injury time, things looked bad. But we kept on going and, three minutes from the end, Anichebe saved the day again. There was a late rescue act in the Fulham game too; Vydra earning us a draw with all of four minutes to go against the Cottagers.

MARCH

Manchester United were looking for revenge when they came to the Black Country in early March and they got it with a 3-0 win as Albion lost Reid, Brunt and Yacob to injury on a grim afternoon.

When we were a goal down at Swansea inside two minutes of our next game, things were looking bad, but we dragged ourselves off the floor in the second half and goals from Sessegnon and Mulumbu in front of a huge travelling Albion support gave us a vital win. Unfortunately, we couldn't repeat it at Hull the following week when Shane Long became a thorn in the side of his old team.

We had another one of those turbo charged starts against Cardiff; Amalfitano and Dorrans giving us a 2-0 lead inside nine minutes, but a lucky goal before the break gave struggling Cardiff hope. They equalised with 17 minutes left but deep into injury time, Thievy won us the game with a clever goal from a Berahino cross. Except he didn't because within seconds, Cardiff were up the other end to equalise.

APRIL

After that, it was beginning to look as if Albion might slip out of the Premier League if we weren't careful. We went to play at Norwich, knowing we had to beat them to leapfrog them in the table. One Amalfitano goal later and things were suddenly feeling much, much better!

We felt even happier when we were 3-0 up at home to Spurs after half an hour, but an unlucky deflection off Jonas Olsson got them back into the game. Twenty minutes from time they got a second, but we looked to be hanging on until, in injury time, Eriksen got an equaliser. Another draw…

With Manchester City hunting down the title, we were beaten at the Etihad, but we knew that a win over West Ham would all but secure our status. It came thanks to a Saido Berahino strike after 11 minutes, the following 80 minutes seeming like hours! But we got there in the end, making the defeats to Arsenal, Sunderland and Stoke that bit easier to bear.

Not a vintage year, but we're still there in the Premier League! And 2014/15 is another year!

Day	Month	Date	Opposition	Score	Crowd	Scorers
Sat	Aug	17	Southampton	0-1	25927	
Sat	Aug	24	Everton	0-0	36410	
Tue	Aug	27	Newport County AFC (C1c2)	3-0	8955	Berahino 3
Sat	Aug	31	Swansea City	0-2	23395	
Sat	Sep	14	Fulham	1-1	25560	McAuley
Sat	Sep	21	Sunderland	3-0	24595	Sessegnon, Ridgewell, Amalfitano
Wed	Sep	25	Arsenal (C1c3)	1-1	18649	Berahino (Arsenal won 4-3 on penalties)
Sat	Sep	28	Manchester United	2-1	75042	Amalfitano, Berahino
Sun	Oct	6	Arsenal	1-1	24839	Yacob
Sat	Oct	19	Stoke City	0-0	25904	
Sat	Oct	26	Liverpool	1-4	44747	Morrison
Sat	Nov	2	Crystal Palace	2-0	26397	Berahino, McAuley
Sat	Nov	9	Chelsea	2-2	41623	Long, Sessegnon
Mon	Nov	25	Aston Villa	2-2	24902	Long 2
Sat	Nov	30	Newcastle United	1-2	49298	Brunt
Wed	Dec	4	Manchester City	2-3	22943	Pantilimon (og), Anichebe
Sat	Dec	7	Norwich City	0-2	23675	
Sat	Dec	14	Cardiff City	0-1	26632	
Sat	Dec	21	Hull City	1-1	24753	Vydra
Thu	Dec	26	Tottenham Hotspur	1-1	35545	Olsson
Sat	Dec	28	West Ham United	3-3	34946	Anelka 2, Berahino
Wed	Jan	1	Newcastle United	1-0	26430	Berahino
Sat	Jan	4	Crystal Palace (FAc3)	0-2	12700	
Sat	Jan	11	Southampton	0-1	28610	
Mon	Jan	20	Everton	1-1	24184	Lugano
Wed	Jan	29	Aston Villa	3-4	36083	Brunt, Delph (og), Mulumbu
Sun	Feb	2	Liverpool	1-1	26132	Anichebe
Sat	Feb	8	Crystal Palace	1-3	24501	Thievy
Tue	Feb	11	Chelsea	1-1	24327	Anichebe
Sat	Feb	22	Fulham	1-1	25782	Vydra
Sat	Mar	8	Manchester United	0-3	26184	
Sat	Mar	15	Swansea City	2-1	20703	Sessegnon, Mulumbu
Sat	Mar	22	Hull City	0-2	23486	
Sat	Mar	29	Cardiff City	3-3	25661	Amalfitano, Dorrans, Thievy
Sat	Apr	5	Norwich City	1-0	26859	Amalfitano
Sat	Apr	12	Tottenham Hotspur	3-3	25398	Vydra, Brunt, Sessegnon
Mon	Apr	21	Manchester City	1-3	46564	Dorrans
Sat	Apr	26	West Ham United	1-0	26541	Berahino
Sun	May	4	Arsenal	0-1	60021	
Wed	May	7	Sunderland	0-2	45181	
Sun	May	11	Stoke City	1-2	26613	Sessegnon

the SEASON in STATS!

PLAYER OF THE SEASON

Ben Foster. He's so good that he managed to miss a third of the 2013/14 season and yet still come out on top of the vote for our player of the season.

When Ben limped off late in our second game of the season, up at Everton's Goodison Park, it looked like a big blow for the Albion.

What we didn't know was that it might have been a bigger blow yet for Ben because it was such a serious injury to his foot that if it hadn't healed properly, it might have put his whole career in danger.

Thankfully, Ben was patient with the injury and just before Christmas, he was back in the team and keeping opposition attackers away from goal.

Not only was he good enough to win our awards, Ben also forced his way back into the England squad and spent his summer out in Brazil at the World Cup.

Good preparation for another award winning season we hope!

QUIZ!
WHERE'S MY PHONE?

Youssouf Mulumbu can't believe it. He can hear his phone ringing, but the players have hidden it in the middle of this maze.

Can you help Youssouf find his phone and answer his calls?

Answer on Page 61

WORDS OF WISDOM

Liverpool were the source for Albion's number 2 this season, defender Andre Wisdom signing for the Throstles from the Anfield club in the summer.

The England Under-21 international spent last season on loan at Sky Bet Championship outfit Derby County, making 34 appearances as the Rams narrowly missed out on promotion, failing to defeat QPR in the play-off final at Wembley. Albion head coach Alan Irvine said, "I've spoken to Brendan Rodgers, who I've known for a very long time and who I trust implicitly. He said Andre would do a good job for us. That was reassuring.

"You want to find out about the person. You can see the player but you want to find out what they are like as a person. Brendan spoke very, very highly about him.

"He's a versatile lad. He's played as a right-back for Liverpool in the Premier League last season; he also played as a full-back for Derby. He grew up as a centre-back and has played on the left side of central defence for Liverpool."

Wisdom began his youth career at Bradford before moving to Anfield at the age of 14. He was named in the England Under-16 side that won the 2008 Victory Shield – and a year later triumphed at the Euro U17 Championships in Liechtenstein, scoring the opening goal in the 2-1 final victory over Spain.

He captained England Under-19s before being handed his Under-21s debut against Israel in September 2011.

Wisdom scored on his Liverpool debut in a 5-3 Europa League victory at Swiss side Young Boys in September 2012. Six days later he made his first domestic start in a 2-1 Capital One Cup win over Albion at The Hawthorns.

Let's hope he plays in lots more winning teams at The Hawthorns!

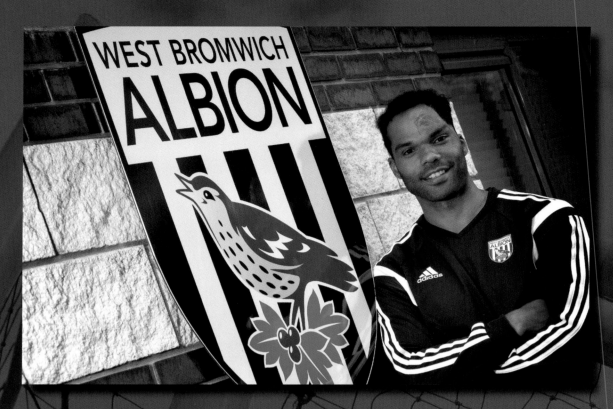

Joleon Lescott swapped the Premier League champions for the Albion this summer when the Baggies beat off competition from many others clubs to get him to sign on at The Hawthorns.

The 31 year old has also played for Wolves and Everton as well as Manchester City. And he also has 26 England caps to his name too.

Joleon became Alan Irvine's first signing after he took over as Head Coach, the two of them having previously worked together at Goodison Park.

"I'm delighted we could bring Joleon to the club," said Irvine.

"He's an England international and a proven Premier League player, who has been at the top level for a number of years.

"He's got Premier League and cup medals to his name and has had a fantastic career so far.

"I know Joleon and the type of personality and character he is, in addition to knowing what he can do as a player.

"He's a great professional and he will add to a number of very good professionals who are already in the squad.

"It's vitally important for me that we don't go into a Premier League season with only three centre-backs at senior level – and I'm delighted with the four proven centre-backs we now have.

"Nobody is guaranteed a place in the team; I have to pick the best two, or sometimes we might play with a three, and I have to work out the ones who can do the best job in any particular game."

Lescott admitted the prospect of being reunited with Alan Irvine was a big factor in his decision to join Albion.

"Working with Alan and knowing how he works from Everton; it was a big thing to be able to come and work with him again.

"At the time, I hadn't played left-back before, and he took the time out to guide me and help me out in any way I needed.

"I was reluctant to play at left-back but I knew I was doing a job for the team and Alan helped me with that. We've stayed in contact throughout the time we haven't worked together.

"And Keith Downing, I've known for years. He was my youth-team manager at Wolves and has been a massive influence on my career. Again, I've spoken to him throughout my career and whenever I've needed advice I'll give him a text or a call.

"Rob Kelly was my youth development officer at Wolves when I first started off. They're all people I admire in the game.

"Knowing them all has made the decision a little bit easier while the location also helps. It all just fell into place nicely."

JOY FOR JOLEON!

QUIZ!
WHICH ONE'S THE REAL BALL?

There were plenty of players in the penalty area when the corner came over, but we've added some more balls to the picture to try and confuse them – can you help them work out which one's the real ball?

Answer on Page 61

TOP SCORER!

SAIDO BERAHINO

Nine goals ensured that Saido ended up as Albion's top scorer in 2013/14 – that gives him plenty to live up to this season doesn't it?!

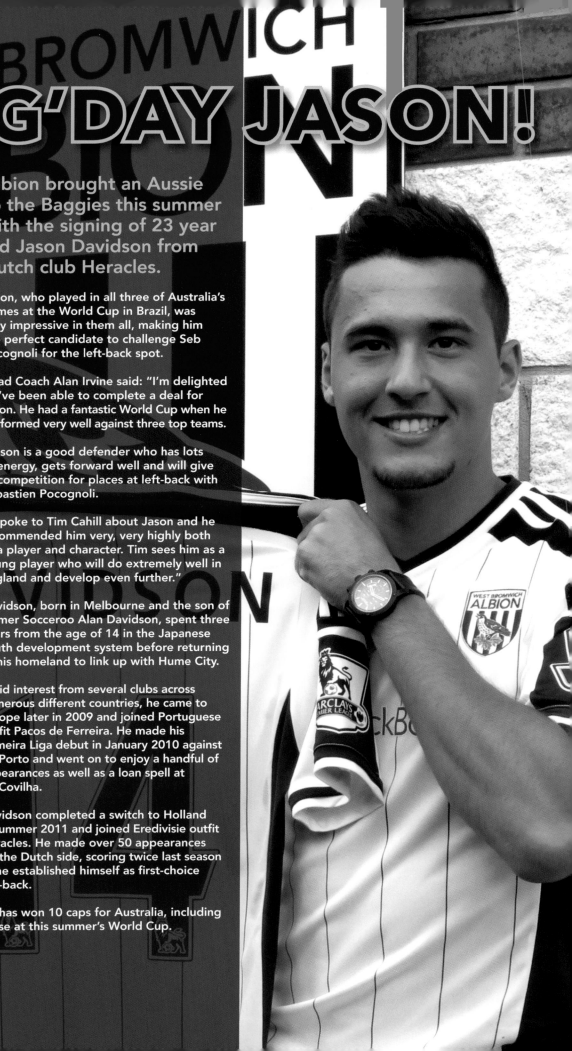

G'DAY JASON!

Albion brought an Aussie to the Baggies this summer with the signing of 23 year old Jason Davidson from Dutch club Heracles.

Jason, who played in all three of Australia's games at the World Cup in Brazil, was very impressive in them all, making him the perfect candidate to challenge Seb Pocognoli for the left-back spot.

Head Coach Alan Irvine said: "I'm delighted we've been able to complete a deal for Jason. He had a fantastic World Cup when he performed very well against three top teams.

"Jason is a good defender who has lots of energy, gets forward well and will give us competition for places at left-back with Sebastien Pocognoli.

"I spoke to Tim Cahill about Jason and he recommended him very, very highly both as a player and character. Tim sees him as a young player who will do extremely well in England and develop even further."

Davidson, born in Melbourne and the son of former Socceroo Alan Davidson, spent three years from the age of 14 in the Japanese youth development system before returning to his homeland to link up with Hume City.

Amid interest from several clubs across numerous different countries, he came to Europe later in 2009 and joined Portuguese outfit Pacos de Ferreira. He made his Primeira Liga debut in January 2010 against FC Porto and went on to enjoy a handful of appearances as well as a loan spell at SC Covilha.

Davidson completed a switch to Holland in summer 2011 and joined Eredivisie outfit Heracles. He made over 50 appearances for the Dutch side, scoring twice last season as he established himself as first-choice left-back.

He has won 10 caps for Australia, including those at this summer's World Cup.

ALBION AT THE WORLD CUP

It might not have been the greatest World Cup on record for England, but Brazil 2014 will go down in the history books at The Hawthorns after Ben Foster became the fifth Albion man to represent England at the World Cup finals.

Ben was following in a fine tradition, begun way back in 1958, when three Albion men (shown left)wore the three lions in the tournament in Sweden. Centre-forward Derek Kevan, right-back Don Howe and inside-forward Bobby Robson all played there, Don and Derek playing in all four of England's games, Bobby playing three. Derek was England's top scorer in the competition, with two of the four goals.

Twelve years later, in 1970, Jeff Astle (above) was on the plane to Mexico, coming on as a substitute against Brazil and then playing from the start against Czechoslovakia.

We had to wait a long, long time before another Throstle made an England World Cup side, but when Ben kept a clean sheet against Costa Rica, it ended 44 years of hurt – for the Albion at least!

QUIZ!
FIND OUR GREAT TEAM!

Somehow, we have managed to lose an entire team of Albion heroes – can you find them all inside this grid?

Words can go horizontally, vertically and diagonally in all eight directions. Answer on Page 61

ASTLE
BARLOW
BATSON
BROWN
JOHNSTON

KENNEDY
OSBORNE
REGIS
ROBSON

STATHAM
WILE

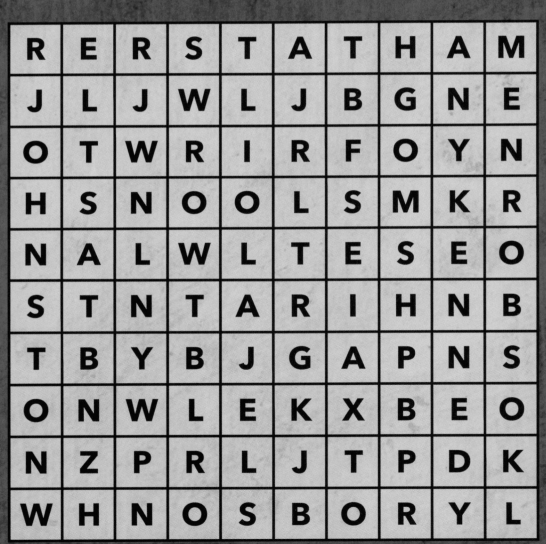

R	E	R	S	T	A	T	H	A	M
J	L	J	W	L	J	B	G	N	E
O	T	W	R	I	R	F	O	Y	N
H	S	N	O	O	L	S	M	K	R
N	A	L	W	L	T	E	S	E	O
S	T	N	T	A	R	I	H	N	B
T	B	Y	B	J	G	A	P	N	S
O	N	W	L	E	K	X	B	E	O
N	Z	P	R	L	J	T	P	D	K
W	H	N	O	S	B	O	R	Y	L

TEAM CAPTAIN
CHRIS BRUNT

Chris Brunt has been the Albion captain ever since Roy Hodgson came here as manager and he has now completed three full seasons with the armband.

At the end of 2013/14, the Northern Irish international was the top appearance maker (249) and top goal scorer (39) at the football club.

No wonder he's our club captain too!

WBA V LIVERPOOL
02-02-2014
THE ALBION
FOUNDATION DAY

WE KNOW HOW TO ENJOY OURSELVES

WHEN THE GOALS GO FLOODING IN, THESE ALBION BOYS KNOW HOW TO CELEBRATE!

QUIZ!
CROSSWORD

Just how well do you know The Hawthorns?

Test your knowledge with the crossword below!

Answers on Page 61

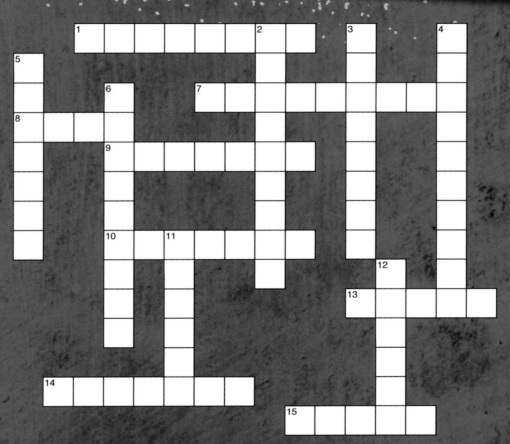

ACROSS

1   Big Vic's surname. (8)
7   He has a statue in The Hawthorns! (4,5)
8   Mr O'Neil. (4)
9   The Club we bought Victor Anichebe from. (7)
10 Where do you go for the FA Cup Final? (7)
13 First name of 2013/14's top scorer. (5)
14 Famous goalscorer from our Three Degrees. (7)
15 Albion's captain. (5)

DOWN

2   England's number one! (3,6)
3   What's the bird on our badge? (8)
4   Where did we get Stephane Sessegnon from? (10)
5   He's better than Kaka! (7)
6   The end of the ground opposite the Brummie! (9)
11 Boaz's surname. (6)
12 Who's in the picture? (6)

HE'S CRAIG, HE'S THE GARDNER!

Albion's first signing of a busy summer was 27 year old midfielder Craig Gardner who joined us on a Bosman transfer after leaving Sunderland.

It meant a long awaited return to the midlands for Solihull born Craig who came through the youth system at Villa Park before joining Birmingham City, winning a League Cup medal with the Blues against Arsenal in 2011.

Over the course of his career, Craig has played 232 games, scoring 31 goals, mostly from midfield although he has also played as a right-back too.

"It's obviously a pleasure to join Albion, it's a great club," Gardner said on arriving at The Hawthorns.

"I've got a lot of friends here from previous clubs like Ben Foster and Stephane Sessegnon and I'm just buzzing that I'm back at home in the Midlands where I enjoy my football the most and where I feel I play my best football.

"I was linked with West Brom previously and I was just praying it happened this time. I'm over the moon.

"People say you have to be happy at home to be happy in your job - and when you've got your friends and family around you encouraging and supporting you then that's when you'll play your best football.

"Thankfully, now I've got that."

WEST BROMWICH ALBION

ALBION PREMIER LEAGUE
DREAM TEAM

The Throstles have completed eight seasons in the Premier League now, so we decided it was time to pick an all-time Albion Premier League team.

We've taken two players from each season to make up a team and five substitutes and we are playing in a 3-5-2 formation.

Who's the head coach? Roy Hodgson of course – he is the England manager after all!

DEFENDER
Jonas Olsson
(2011/2)

GOALKEEPER
Ben Foster
(2013/4)

DEFENDER
Curtis Davies
(2005/6)

DEFENDER
Gareth McAuley
(2013/4)

SUBSTITUTES

GOALKEEPER
Russell Hoult (2004/5)

DEFENDER
Darren Moore (2002/3)

MIDFIELDER
Robert Koren (2008/9)

MIDFIELDER
Zoltan Gera (2005/6)

STRIKER
Robert Earnshaw (2004/5)

LEFT WING BACK
Chris Brunt
(2008/9)

MIDFIELDER
James Morrison
(2011/2)

STRIKER
Romelu Lukaku
(2012/3)

MIDFIELDER
Claudio Yacob
(2012/3)

STRIKER
Peter Odemwingie
(2010/1)

MIDFIELDER
Youssouf Mulumbu
(2010/1)

RIGHT WING BACK
Igor Balis
(2002/3)

THE LOOK OF THE IRISH!

Northern Irish international Chris Baird joined Albion in the summer and was quick to tell everyone what he's come for – he's here to help!

The former Fulham man is determined to make the most of his return to the Barclays Premier League after spending last term in the Championship with Reading and Burnley.

"All the staff have been very welcoming and I've settled in quickly," said Baird.

"Albion have been in for me before, I know a few of the lads here and I'm really looking forward to the challenge. I want to enjoy the Premier League again.

"When I left Fulham it was tough going back to the Championship - the leagues are totally different. When this opportunity came around I wanted to take it.

"I don't mind where I play; I'm here to help out in any way I can, whether it's left-back or right-back, centre-half or centre-midfield. I can play all those positions.

"Some people say it's nice to have that versatility but sometimes it is frustrating because you can't nail down that one position.

"But it's up to the head coach where he wants to play me."

Head coach Alan Irvine said, "Chris is a player with vast Premier League and international experience who reads the game well and has good positional sense.

"He can play in several positions and his versatility effectively makes your squad bigger. It's important we have the right characters in the dressing room and Chris is certainly that.

"We have done our homework on him. I have spoken to a lot of different people who have either managed or played with Chris and everyone spoke very, very highly of him both as a player and a person."

WEST BROMWICH
ALBION

VICTOR
ANICHEBE

QUIZ!
HOME NATIONS

Here are four Albion players who have represented the home nations at one level or another.

But which player goes with which country?

Ben Foster

Graham Dorrans

Gareth McAuley

Boaz Myhill

Choose from the following countries:

1. **Northern Ireland**   2. **Wales**   3. **Scotland**   4. **England**

Answer on Page 61

ONWARD CRISTIAN SOLDIER!

Costa Rica came to Albion this summer with the arrival of Cristian Gamboa at the Hawthorns.

Cristian was brought to everyone's attention as part of the Costa Rica team who had such a great World Cup in Brazil, qualifying on top of the group containing Uruguay, Italy and England.

The right-back joined Albion from Rosenborg of Norway, desperate to make a name for himself in the Premier League.

"For me, the move is a dream come true, I feel really happy because it is the biggest step of my career," the 24-year-old said.

"It is a good moment, also after the World Cup, I am happy to be here and I hope the people at West Bromwich Albion will like how I play - and my performances.

"Albion were one of the first clubs to show an interest in me so I believe in the work they are doing.

"It is a big step for me to be here, it is a big step to be in the Premier League, it is really important to have a club where you can play and show your skills.

"For me, it is the right club to play in the Premier League."

QUIZ!

BUILD AROUND CLAUDIO YACOB!

Like the Albion, we have Claudio Yacob in the middle here, but can you fill in all the blanks around him to complete this Albion quiz?

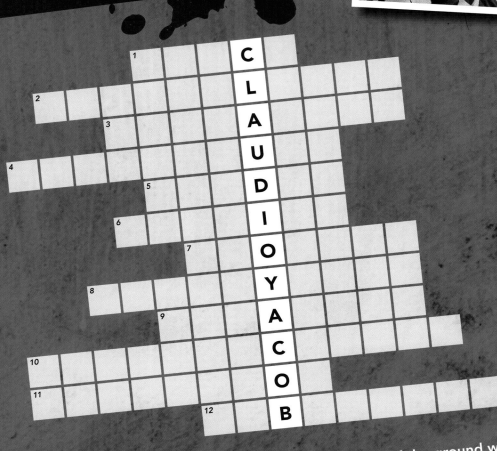

1. It's what we grow the grass on.

2. Albion's Swedish international defender.

3. The man who scored the FA Cup winner in 1968.

4. Albion's club captain.

5. The company that makes our kit

6. Come on you _____!

7. The corner of the ground where the Throstle is perched.

8. He wears number 13.

9. Albion's young goalscorer, Saido _____.

10. Northern Irish centre-half.

11. He came from Sunderland, Stephane _____.

12. This former Albion goalscorer had a super nickname!

Answers on Page 61

WEST BROMWICH
ALBION

JONAS
OLSSON

THE OPPOSITION

There are 19 teams aiming to do better than us in the Premier League this season – we'd better find out about them then shouldn't we?

CRYSTAL PALACE:

Stadium: Selhurst Park

Nickname: The Eagles

Record league win: 9-0 v Barrow, 10 October 1959

Record league defeat: 0-9 v Liverpool, 12 September 1989

EVERTON:

Stadium: Goodison Park

Nickname: The Toffees

Record league win: 9-1 v Manchester City, 3 September 1906 & v Plymouth Argyle, 27 December 1930

Record league defeat: 0-7 v Sunderland, 26 December 1934, v Wolves 22 February 1939 & v Arsenal 11 May 2005

HULL CITY:

Stadium: KC Stadium

Nickname: The Tigers

Record league win: 11-1 v Carlisle United, 14 January 1939

Record league defeat: 0-8 v Wolves, 4 November 1911

LEICESTER CITY:

Stadium: King Power Stadium

Nickname: The Foxes

Record league win: 10-0 v Portsmouth, 20 October 1928

Record league defeat: 0-12 v Nottingham Forest, 21 April 1909

ARSENAL:

Stadium: The Emirates

Nickname: The Gunners

Record league win: 12-0 v Loughborough, 12 March 1900

Record league defeat: 0-8 v Loughborough, 12 December 1896

ASTON VILLA:

Stadium: Villa Park

Nickname: The Villans

Record league win: 12-2 v Accrington, 12 March 1892

Record league defeat: 0-8 v Chelsea, 23 December 2012

BURNLEY:

Stadium: Turf Moor

Nickname: The Clarets

Record league win: 9-0 v Darwen, 9 January 1892

Record league defeat: 0-10 v Aston Villa, 29 August 1925

CHELSEA:

Stadium: Stamford Bridge

Nickname: The Pensioners

Record league win: 8-0 v Wigan Athletic, 9 May 2010 & v Aston Villa, 23 December 2012

Record league defeat: 1-8 v Wolves, 26 September 1953

LIVERPOOL:

Stadium: Anfield

Nickname: The Reds

Record league win: 10-1 v Rotherham Town, 18 February 1896

Record league defeat: 1-9 v Birmingham City, 11 December 1954

MANCHESTER CITY:

Stadium: The Etihad Stadium

Nickname: The Citizens

Record league win: 11-3 v Lincoln City, 23 March 1895

Record league defeat: 1-9 v Everton, 3 September 1906

MANCHESTER UNITED:

Stadium: Old Trafford

Nickname: The Red Devils

Record league win: 10-1 v Wolves, 15 October 1892

Record league defeat: 0-7 v Blackburn Rovers, 10 April 1926, v Aston Villa, 27 December 1930 & v Wolves 26 December 1931

NEWCASTLE UNITED:

Stadium: St James' Park

Nickname: The Magpies

Record league win: 13-0 v Newport County, 5 October 1946

Record league defeat: 0-9 v Burton Wanderers, 15 April 1895

QUEENS PARK RANGERS:

Stadium: Loftus Road

Nickname: The R's

Record league win: 9-2 v Tranmere Rovers, 3 December 1960

Record league defeat: 1-8 v Manchester United, 19 March 1969

SOUTHAMPTON:

Stadium: St Mary's Stadium

Nickname: The Saints

Record league win: 9-3 v Wolves, 18 September 1965

Record league defeat: 0-8 v Tottenham Hotspur, 28 March 1936 & v Everton, 20 November 1971

STOKE CITY:

Stadium: The Britannia Stadium

Nickname: The Potters

Record league win: 10-3 v West Bromwich Albion, 4 February 1937

Record league defeat: 0-10 v Preston North End, 14 September 1889

SUNDERLAND:

Stadium: The Sunderland Stadium of Light

Nickname: The Black Cats

Record league win: 9-1 v Newcastle United, 5 December 1908

Record league defeat: 0-8 v Sheffield Wednesday, 26 December 1911, v West Ham United, 19 October 1968 & v Watford, 25 September 1982

SWANSEA CITY:

Stadium: The Liberty Stadium

Nickname: The Swans

Record league win: 8-1 v Bristol Rovers, 15 April 1922, v Bradford City, 22 February 1936 & v Hartlepool United, 1 April 1978

Record league defeat: 1-8 v Fulham, 22 January 1938

TOTTENHAM HOTSPUR:

Stadium: White Hart Lane

Nickname: The Lilywhites

Record league win: 9-0 v Bristol Rovers, 22 October 1977

Record league defeat: 2-8 v Derby County, 16 October 1976

WEST HAM UNITED:

Stadium: The Boleyn Ground

Nickname: The Hammers

Record league win: 8-0 v Rotherham United, 8 March 1958 & v Sunderland, 19 October 1968

Record league defeat: 0-7 v Barnsley, 1 September 1919, v Everton 22 October 1927 & v Sheffield 28 November 1959

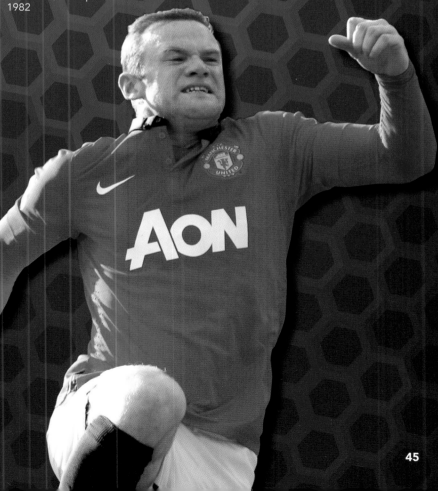

WHERE IS MY BADGE?!

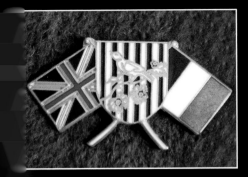

Throughout the years, lots of badges, pennants and even handkerchiefs, have been issued. Some official, some not so much – all about the Albion.

They might not seem very much at the time, fiddly little things, but over the years they become more and more important. Reminders of great cup wins or just great days out at the Albion.

You could even start your own collection? Perhaps pin them to your Albion scarf? Just make sure your mum doesn't have a clear-out one day!

ALL THAT JAZZ!

The Albion News, Albion's matchday programme, went jazz crazy last season with our design and covers inspired by lots of famous record sleeves from years ago – ask your granddad!

What will the cover theme be for the new season? There's only one way to find out – make sure you buy a copy of Albion News at every game!

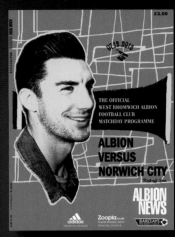

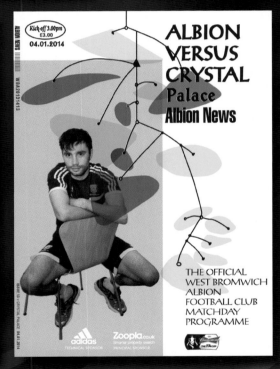

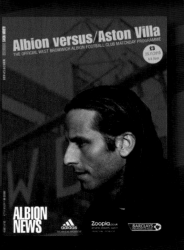

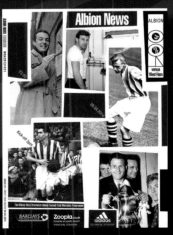

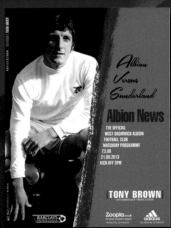

GOOD ADVICE!

Albion's Belgian left-back was persuaded to join the Baggies after getting some good advice from a former Albion hero, Romelu Lukaku.

Seb Pocognoli, who has signed a three-year deal, plus a year's option in the club's favour, said, "My mate Romelu Lukaku played here. I've tried to follow his career for the last two years, so I know a little bit about the club and its history from his time here.

"I spoke to him and he's the person who can give me the best opinion of the club. He was very, very positive. He said that if I had the opportunity to come here then I had to.

"His experience here was great. He told me that his relationship with the supporters was very good."

Seb says he is excited to have joined the Baggies from Hannover 96 in the Bundesliga.

"To play in England was always my dream, I was always working towards that. I'm very happy to be here and I just want to prove my quality."

Head coach Alan Irvine said, "Sébastien is an experienced left-back who has played at a high level for many years. After being named in Belgium's provisional World Cup squad, he just missed out on Brazil, mainly because he hadn't played enough games towards the end of the season.

"But he's joined us with a real hunger to prove himself at Albion and get back into the international set-up. We've talked to people who have worked with him, including Romelu Lukaku and Kevin Mirallas.

"You make your own mind up about a player's ability from watching him play but you put these calls in to find out about their personality. The word on Sébastien was very positive."

RECORD BREAKER!

He is Albion's record signing; he follows in the footsteps of another great Nigerian goal scorer, AND he shares a name with our greatest ever player – Tony Brown. What better omens could there be for Brown Ideye?!

Costa Rica came to the Albion this summer. The 25 year old came to The Hawthorns in the summer 2014, leaving Dynamo Kiev to fulfil his dream of playing in England's Premier League and immediately taking on the number nine shirt worn in the past by greats such as Jeff Astle, Cyrille Regis and Bob Taylor.

Brown has played in the Champions League in the past and has a total of 74 goals in 182 league games over his career before he arrived at the Albion.

Alan Irvine tells us that, "Brown is a quality striker. He's a strong, quick, powerful player who likes to get in behind defences and has plenty of Champions League and international experience."

Technical director Terry Burton added, "Brown was the man at the top of our wish list. It is a fantastic signing because of the quality and the potential of the player. I can see that he really wants to be here and that he really wants to be playing in the Premier League. He's a dynamic player who likes to get in behind defenders and he has the pace to do so. He gets himself into good scoring positions in the box and if there are opportunities then he will get on the end of them."

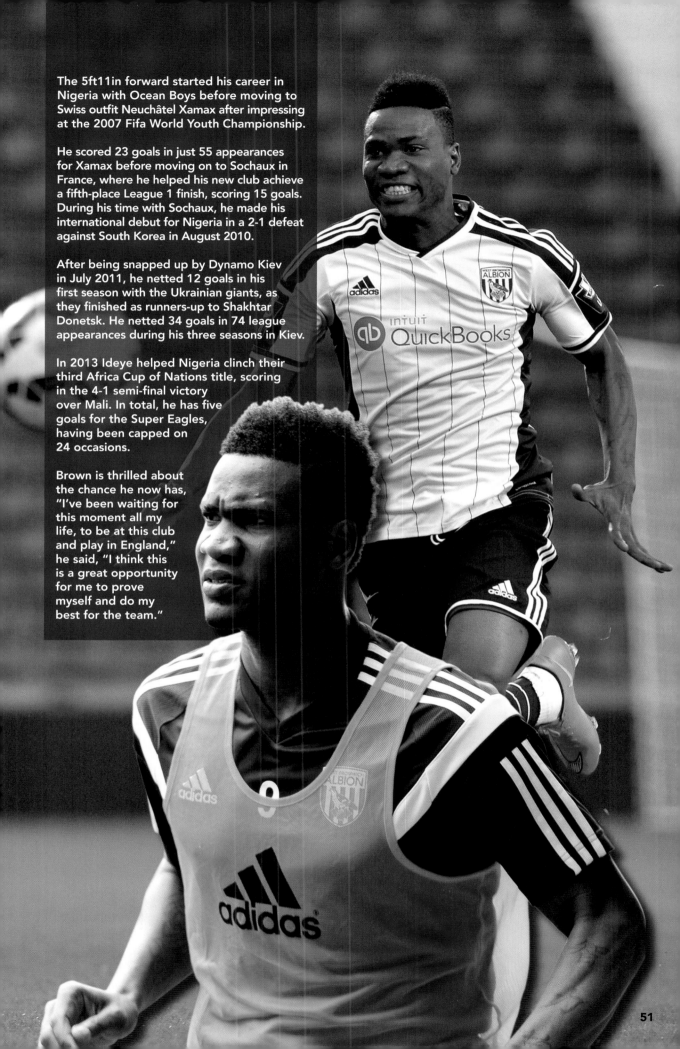

The 5ft11in forward started his career in Nigeria with Ocean Boys before moving to Swiss outfit Neuchâtel Xamax after impressing at the 2007 Fifa World Youth Championship.

He scored 23 goals in just 55 appearances for Xamax before moving on to Sochaux in France, where he helped his new club achieve a fifth-place League 1 finish, scoring 15 goals. During his time with Sochaux, he made his international debut for Nigeria in a 2-1 defeat against South Korea in August 2010.

After being snapped up by Dynamo Kiev in July 2011, he netted 12 goals in his first season with the Ukrainian giants, as they finished as runners-up to Shakhtar Donetsk. He netted 34 goals in 74 league appearances during his three seasons in Kiev.

In 2013 Ideye helped Nigeria clinch their third Africa Cup of Nations title, scoring in the 4-1 semi-final victory over Mali. In total, he has five goals for the Super Eagles, having been capped on 24 occasions.

Brown is thrilled about the chance he now has, "I've been waiting for this moment all my life, to be at this club and play in England," he said, "I think this is a great opportunity for me to prove myself and do my best for the team."

PLAYER PROFILES

BEN FOSTER

Birthdate:	3 April 1983
Position:	Goalkeeper
Height:	1.93m
Weight:	90kg
Other clubs:	Stafford Rangers, Stoke City, Manchester United, Birmingham City
Albion games:	94
Albion goals:	0

BOAZ MYHILL

Birthdate:	9 November 1982
Position:	Goalkeeper
Height:	1.91m
Weight:	92kg
Other clubs:	Aston Villa, Hull City
Albion games:	36
Albion goals:	0

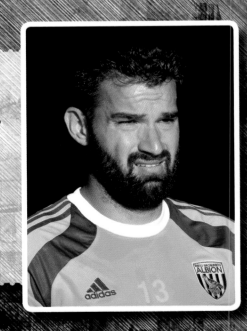

JONAS OLSSON

Birthdate:	10 March 1983
Position:	Centre-half
Height:	1.93m
Weight:	84kg
Other clubs:	Landskrona, NEC Nijmegen
Albion games:	204+1
Albion goals:	12

GARETH McAULEY

Birthdate:	5 December 1979
Position:	Centre-half
Height:	1.95m
Weight:	90kg
Other clubs:	Coleraine, Lincoln City, Leicester City, Ipswich Town
Albion games:	106+1
Albion goals:	7

ANDRE WISDOM

Birthdate:	9 May 1983
Position:	Defender
Height:	1.86cm
Weight:	78kg
Other clubs:	Liverpool
Albion games:	0
Albion goals:	0

CRAIG DAWSON

Birthdate:	6 May 1990
Position:	Centre-half
Height:	1.88m
Weight:	85kg
Other clubs:	Rochdale
Albion games:	24+7
Albion goals:	0

JASON DAVIDSON

Birthdate:	29 June 1991
Position:	Defender
Height:	1.80cm
Weight:	72kg
Other clubs:	Hume City, Pacos de Ferreira, Heracles Almelo
Albion games:	0
Albion goals:	0

CRISTIAN GAMBOA

Birthdate:	24 October 1989
Position:	Defender
Height:	1.75m
Weight:	67kg
Other clubs:	Municipal Liberia, Fredrikstad, Copenhagen, Rosenborg
Albion games:	0
Albion goals:	0

JOLEON LESCOTT

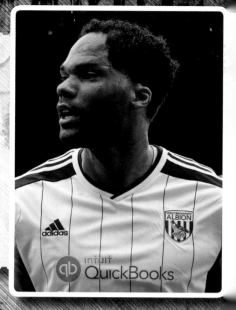

Birthdate:	16 August 1982
Position:	Central defender
Height:	1.88cm
Weight:	82kg
Other clubs:	Wolves, Everton, Manchester City
Albion games:	0
Albion goals:	0

LIAM O'NEIL

Birthdate:	31 July 1993
Position:	Defender
Height:	1.83cm
Weight:	79kg
Albion games:	0+3
Albion goals:	0

CHRIS BAIRD

Birthdate:	25 February 1982
Position:	Defender
Height:	1.85cm
Weight:	73kg
Other clubs:	Southampton, Fulham, Reading, Burnley
Albion games:	0
Albion goals:	0

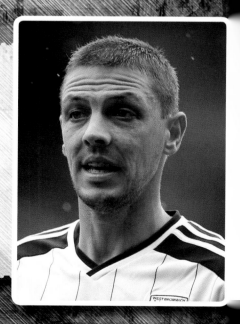

SEBASTIEN POCOGNOLI

Birthdate:	1 August 1987
Position:	Defender
Height:	1.82m
Weight:	73kg
Other clubs:	Genk, AZ Alkmaar, Standard Liege, Hannover 96
Albion games:	0
Albion goals:	0

CLAUDIO YACOB

Birthdate:	18 July 1987
Position:	Central midfielder
Height:	1.81m
Weight:	73kg
Other clubs:	Racing Club de Avellaneda
Albion games:	53+6
Albion goals:	1

CHRIS BRUNT

Birthdate:	14 December 1984
Position:	Winger
Height:	1.87m
Weight:	85kg
Other clubs:	Sheffield Wednesday
Albion games:	210+39
Albion goals:	39

GRAHAM DORRANS

Birthdate:	5 May 1987
Position:	Midfielder
Height:	1.79m
Weight:	78kg
Other clubs:	Livingston
Albion games:	131+35
Albion goals:	25

YOUSSOUF MULUMBU

Birthdate:	25 January 1987
Position:	Central midfielder
Height:	1.74m
Weight:	76kg
Other clubs:	Paris St-Germain
Albion games:	172+18
Albion goals:	15

JAMES MORRISON

Birthdate:	25 May 1986
Position:	Central midfielder
Height:	1.80m
Weight:	75kg
Other clubs:	Middlesbrough
Albion games:	177+45
Albion goals:	24

CRAIG GARDNER

Birthdate:	25 November 1986
Position:	Central midfielder
Height:	1.76cm
Weight:	81kg
Other clubs:	Aston Villa, Birmingham City, Sunderland
Albion games:	0
Albion goals:	0

VICTOR ANICHEBE

Birthdate:	23 April 1988
Position:	Striker
Height:	1.91m
Weight:	80kg
Other clubs:	Everton
Albion games:	11+13
Albion goals:	3

STEPHANE SESSEGNON

Birthdate:	1 June 1984
Position:	Attacking midfiielder
Height:	1.68m
Weight:	75kg
Other clubs:	Requins de l'Atlantique, Créteil, Le Mans, Paris St-Germain, Sunderland
Albion games:	24+4
Albion goals:	5

SAIDO BERAHINO

Birthdate:	4 August 1993
Position:	Striker
Height:	1.80m
Weight:	82kg
Albion games:	14+22
Albion goals:	9

BROWN IDEYE

Birthdate:	10 October 1988
Position:	Striker
Height:	1.80cm
Weight:	70kg
Other clubs:	Ocean Boys, Neuchâtel Xamax, Sochaux, Dynamo Kiev
Albion games:	0
Albion goals:	0

COLOUR ME ALBION!

The rain was so heavy during the match, it washed all the colour out of Jonas Olsson's kit!

Can you cheer him up and give him a properly coloured shirt please?

MAZE, Page 22

CROSSWORD, Page 34

```
        A N I C H E B E       T       S
    M           E             H       U
    U       S       T O N Y B R O W N D
    L I A M         F       R         E
    U       E V E R T O N    O         R
    M       T         S       T         L
    B       H         T       L         A
    U       W E M B L E Y     E   D   N
            I   Y           S A I D O
            C   H           A         D
            K   I           W
                L   C Y R I L L E   S
                L           O       O
                            B R U N T N
```

WHICH ONE'S THE REAL BALL?, Page 26

HOME NATIONS, Page 40

Ben Foster – 4. England
Graham Dorrans – 3. Scotland
Gareth McAuley – 1. Northern Ireland
Boaz Myhill – 2. Wales

FIND OUR GREAT TEAM!, Page 30

```
R E R S T A T H A M
J L J W L J B G N E
O T W R I R F O Y N
H S N O O L S M K R
N A L W L T E S E O
S T N T A R I H N B
T B Y B J G A P N S
O N W L E K X B E O
N Z P R L J T P D K
W H N O S B O R Y L
```

BUILD AROUND CLAUDIO YACOB!, Page 42

1. **Pitch**
2. **Jonas Olsson**
3. **Jeff Astle;**
4. **Chris Brunt**
5. **Adidas**
6. **Baggies;**
7. **Woodman**
8. **Boaz Myhill**
9. **Berahino**
10. **Gareth Mcauley**
11. **Sessegnon;**
12. **Bob Taylor**

WHERE'S BAGGIE?

Baggie Bird is hiding in amongst the fans, can you find him?